TEACHER'S PET PUBLICATIONS

LITPLAN TEACHER PACK
for
The Pearl
based on the book by
John Steinbeck

Written by
Mary B. Collins

© 1996 Teacher's Pet Publications
All Rights Reserved

This **LitPlan** for John Steinbeck's
The Pearl
has been brought to you by Teacher's Pet Publications, Inc.

Copyright Teacher's Pet Publications 1996
11504 Hammock Point
Berlin MD 21811

Only the student materials in this unit plan
such as worksheets, study questions, assignment sheets and tests
may be reproduced multiple times for use in the purchaser's classroom.

For any additional copyright questions,
contact Teacher's Pet Publications.

www.tpet.com

TABLE OF CONTENTS - *The Pearl*

Introduction	5
Unit Objectives	8
Reading Assignment Sheet	9
Unit Outline	10
Study Questions (Short Answer)	13
Quiz/Study Questions (Multiple Choice)	18
Pre-reading Vocabulary Worksheets	29
Lesson One (Introductory Lesson)	41
Nonfiction Assignment Sheet	43
Oral Reading Evaluation Form	45
Writing Assignment 1	47
Writing Assignment 2	53
Writing Assignment 3	58
Writing Evaluation Form	56
Vocabulary Review Activities	51
Extra Writing Assignments/Discussion ?s	50
Unit Review Activities	60
Unit Tests	63
Unit Resource Materials	89
Vocabulary Resource Materials	101

A FEW NOTES ABOUT THE AUTHOR
JOHN STEINBECK

STEINBECK, John (1902-68). Winner of the 1962 Nobel prize for literature, the American author John Steinbeck is best remembered for his novel 'The Grapes of Wrath'. Steinbeck's story of a family of farm workers migrating from Oklahoma to California describes the hopelessness of the Great Depression era.

John Ernst Steinbeck was born on Feb. 27, 1902, in Salinas, Calif. He took classes at Stanford University for several years but left without a degree. He worked as a laborer to support himself while he wrote. Steinbeck's first novel was published in 1929, but it was not until the publication of 'Tortilla Flat' in 1935 that he attained critical and popular acclaim.

He followed this success with 'In Dubious Battle' (1936) and 'Of Mice and Men' (1937). 'The Grapes of Wrath' (1939) earned for Steinbeck a Pulitzer prize. In these works Steinbeck's proletarian themes are expressed through his portrayal of the inarticulate, dispossessed laborers who populate his American landscape. Both 'Of Mice and Men' and 'The Grapes of Wrath' were made into motion pictures.

In 1943 Steinbeck traveled to North Africa and Italy as a war correspondent. Some of his later works include 'Cannery Row' (1945), 'The Pearl' (1947), 'East of Eden' (1952), 'The Winter of Our Discontent' (1961), and 'Travels with Charley' (1962). He also wrote several motion-picture scripts, including adaptations of two of his shorter works-'The Pearl' and 'The Red Pony'. Steinbeck died in New York City on Dec. 20, 1968.

--- Courtesy of Compton's Learning Company

INTRODUCTION

This unit has been designed to develop students' reading, writing, thinking, and language skills through exercises and activities related to *The Pearl* by John Steinbeck. It includes eighteen lessons, supported by extra resource materials.

The **introductory lesson** introduces students to one main theme of the novel through a bulletin board activity. Following the introductory activity, students are given a transition to explain how the activity relates to the book they are about to read. Following the transition, students are given the materials they will be using during the unit. At the end of the lesson, students begin the pre-reading work for the first reading assignment.

The **reading assignments** are approximately thirty pages each; some are a little shorter while others are a little longer. Students have approximately 15 minutes of pre-reading work to do prior to each reading assignment. This pre-reading work involves reviewing the study questions for the assignment and doing some vocabulary work for 8 to 10 vocabulary words they will encounter in their reading.

The **study guide questions** are fact-based questions; students can find the answers to these questions right in the text. These questions come in two formats: short answer required or multiple choice-matching-true/false. The best use of these materials is probably to use the short answer version of the questions as study guides for students (since answers will be more complete), and to use the multiple choice version for occasional quizzes. If your school has the appropriate equipment, it might be a good idea to make transparencies of your answer keys for the overhead projector.

The **vocabulary work** is intended to enrich students' vocabularies as well as to aid in the students' understanding of the book. Prior to each reading assignment, students will complete a two-part worksheet for approximately 8 to 10 vocabulary words in the upcoming reading assignment. Part I focuses on students' use of general knowledge and contextual clues by giving the sentence in which the word appears in the text. Students are then to write down what they think the words mean based on the words' usage. Part II nails down the definitions of the words by giving students dictionary definitions of the words and having students match the words to the correct definitions based on the words' contextual usage. Students should then have a thorough understanding of the words when they meet them in the text.

After each reading assignment, students will go back and formulate answers for the study guide questions. Discussion of these questions serves as a **review** of the most important events and ideas presented in the reading assignments.

After students complete reading the work, a lesson is devoted to the **extra discussion questions/writing assignments**. These questions focus on interpretation, critical analysis and personal response, employing a variety of thinking skills and adding to the students' understanding of the novel.

Following the discussion session, there is a **vocabulary review** lesson which pulls together all of the fragmented vocabulary lists for the reading assignments and gives students a review of all of the words they have studied.

The **group activity** which follows the discussion questions has students working in small groups to discuss the main themes of the novel. Using the information they have acquired so far through individual work and class discussions, students get together to further examine the text and to brainstorm ideas relating to the themes of the novel.

The group activity is followed by a **reports and discussion** session in which the groups share their ideas about the themes with the entire class; thus, the entire class is exposed to information about all of the themes and the entire class can discuss each theme based on the nucleus of information brought forth by each of the groups.

There are three **writing assignments** in this unit, each with the purpose of informing, persuading, or having students express personal opinions. The first assignment is to express personal opinions: students write a composition detailing how they would use their money to make their hopes and dreams come true, if they would become rich overnight like Kino did. The second assignment is to persuade: students pretend they are Juana with Kino and Coyotito in cave before the trackers come. They are to write a composition in which they say what Juana would say to Kino to persuade him to leave the cave, go home, and throw away the pearl. The third assignment is to inform: students write a summary and their opinions of nonfiction articles they have read relating to *The Pearl*.

There is a **nonfiction reading assignment**. Students are required to read a piece of nonfiction related in some way to *The Pearl* (articles about prejudice or coming of age, trial transcripts, etc.). After reading their nonfiction pieces, students will fill out a worksheet on which they answer questions regarding facts, interpretation, criticism, and personal opinions. During one class period, students make **oral presentations** about the nonfiction pieces they have read. This not only exposes all students to a wealth of information, it also gives students the opportunity to practice **public speaking**.

The **review lesson** pulls together all of the aspects of the unit. The teacher is given four or five choices of activities or games to use which all serve the same basic function of reviewing all of the information presented in the unit.

The **unit test** comes in two formats: all multiple choice-matching-true/false or with a mixture of matching, short answer, multiple choice, and composition. As a convenience, two different tests for each format have been included.

There are additional **support materials** included with this unit. The **extra activities** section includes suggestions for an in-class library, crossword and word search puzzles related to the novel, and extra vocabulary worksheets. There is a list of **bulletin board ideas** which gives the teacher suggestions for bulletin boards to go along with this unit. In addition, there is a list of **extra class activities** the teacher could choose from to enhance the unit or as a substitution for an exercise the teacher might feel is inappropriate for his/her class. **Answer keys** are located directly after the **reproducible student materials** throughout the unit. The student materials may be reproduced for use in the teacher's classroom without infringement of copyrights. No other portion of this unit may be reproduced without the written consent of Teacher's Pet Publications, Inc.

UNIT OBJECTIVES - *The Pearl*

1. Through reading John Steinbeck's *The Pearl*, students will gain a better understanding of the themes of good versus evil, the corruption of man, and the inherent goodness of the natural world.

2. Students will demonstrate their understanding of the text on four levels: factual, interpretive, critical and personal.

3. Students will consider their own hopes and dreams for the future.

4. Students will be given the opportunity to practice reading aloud and silently to improve their skills in each area.

5. Students will answer questions to demonstrate their knowledge and understanding of the main events and characters in *The Pearl* as they relate to the author's theme development.

6. Students will enrich their vocabularies and improve their understanding of the novel through the vocabulary lessons prepared for use in conjunction with the novel.

7. The writing assignments in this unit are geared to several purposes:
    a. To have students demonstrate their abilities to inform, to persuade, or to express their own personal ideas
       Note: Students will demonstrate ability to write effectively to <u>inform</u> by developing and organizing facts to convey information. Students will demonstrate the ability to write effectively to <u>persuade</u> by selecting and organizing relevant information, establishing an argumentative purpose, and by designing an appropriate strategy for an identified audience. Students will demonstrate the ability to write effectively to <u>express personal ideas</u> by selecting a form and its appropriate elements.
    b. To check the students' reading comprehension
    c. To make students think about the ideas presented by the novel
    d. To encourage logical thinking
    e. To provide an opportunity to practice good grammar and improve students' use of the English language.

8. Students will read aloud, report, and participate in large and small group discussions to improve their public speaking and personal interaction skills.

READING ASSIGNMENT SHEET - *The Pearl*

Date Assigned	Reading Assignment (Chapters)	Completion Date
	1 & 2	
	3	
	4 & 5	
	6	

UNIT OUTLINE - *The Pearl*

1 Introduction PV 1-2	2 Read 1-2	3 Study ?s 1-2 PVR 3	4 Study ?s 3 Writing Assignment 1 PV 4-5	5 Read 4-5
6 Study ?s 4-5 PVR 6	7 Study ?s 6 Extra Questions	8 Vocabulary	9 Writing Assignment 2	10 Group Activity
11 Activity	12 Library	13 Writing Assignment 3	14 Nonfiction Reports	15 Review
16 Test				

Key: P = Preview Study Questions V = Vocabulary Work R = Read

STUDY GUIDE QUESTIONS

SHORT ANSWER STUDY GUIDE QUESTIONS - *The Pearl*

Chapter 1
1. What, in general, happens in the first chapter?
2. Notice that the townspeople follow Kino. What does that tell you?
3. Why did the doctor refuse to treat Coyotito?
4. What does that tell you about the doctor's personality?
5. What are the conflicts in the story so far?
6. What is the Song of the Family?
7. What is the Song of Evil? When does it first appear?

Chapter 2
1. Why did Steinbeck include the first section about the life in the Gulf waters?
2. The canoe is mentioned quite often. Is it a symbol for something?
3. What is the main event of this chapter?
4. Do you think it is coincidence that everything goes well on the water, or is Steinbeck trying to show something?
5. To what new Song are we introduced?

Chapter 3
1. To what does Steinbeck compare the town?
2. The news of Kino's pearl spread quickly across town. What did each person think of when he heard it?
3. What would Kino do with his riches?
4. Why does the doctor come? What does he do?
5. What bad thing happened to make Juana want to throw away the pearl?

Chapter 4
1. In the description of the pearl buyers, what do we find out about the market in Kino's village?
2. What happened when Kino went to sell his pearl?
3. Juan Tomas says to Kino, "You have defied not the pearl buyers, but the whole structure, the whole way of life. I am afraid for you." What does he mean?
4. Again at the end of the chapter, Juana wants to throw away the pearl because it is evil. What evil thing happened?

Chapter 5
1. Where did Juana go early in the morning?
2. What did Kino do when he figured out where she went?
3. What happened to Kino up the beach through the brushline on the path?
4. What happened to their hut while they were away?
5. Why did they leave the village?

Chapter 6
1. What "songs" does Kino hear on the first part of their journey?
2. What made the music of the pearl become "sinister in his ears, . . . interwoven with the music of evil?"
3. What happens to Coyotito?
4. What happens to the trackers?
5. What happens to Kino and Juana?
6. What do they do with the pearl?
7. What does the return of Kino and Juana and their throwing away the pearl mean symbolically?

KEY: STUDY GUIDE QUESTIONS - *The Pearl*

Chapter 1

1. What, in general, happens in the first chapter?
    Kino and Juana wake up, and prepare for the day. The scorpion strikes Coyotito. They call for the doctor, but the doctor refuses to come. They go to the doctor, but he refuses to treat Coyotito.

2. Notice that the townspeople follow Kino. What does that tell you?
    It tells us two things: the people were curious and the people liked Kino and his family.

3. Why did the doctor refuse to treat Coyotito?
    To the doctor, Coyotito was an Indian "animal." Also, Kino could not pay the doctor well for his services.

4. What does that tell you about the doctor's personality?
    The doctor is not a caring individual. He is materialistic and cold-hearted. He is a doctor for the title, social position and money, not at heart.

5. What are the conflicts in the story so far?
    The conflicts are man vs. man, man vs. society, and man vs. nature.

6. What is the Song of the Family?
    The Song of the Family is a song of happiness, of being "whole." It is a song of peaceful existence, of being together in harmony with the family.

7. What is the Song of Evil? When does it first appear?
    The Song of Evil is a song of disruption, of evil, of the breaking of happiness. It first appears with the scorpion.

Chapter 2

1. Why did Steinbeck include the first section about the life in the Gulf waters?
    This section shows the natural world of which Kino is a part. It shows the old way of survival of the fittest.

2. The canoe is mentioned quite often. Is it a symbol for something?
    Yes. It symbolizes the old way of life, tradition. It was Kino's grandfather's canoe. It shows the continuance of the primitive family.

3. What is the main event of this chapter?
    Kino and Juana find the pearl.

4. Do you think it is coincidence that everything goes well on the water, or is Steinbeck trying to show something?

   In the hands of Kino and Juana alone in nature, the pearl represents happiness and good. We will later see that when they bring it near civilization (the unnatural), it is very, very bad.

5. To what new Song are we introduced?

   We are introduced to the Song of the Pearl That Might Be.

Chapter 3

1. To what does Steinbeck compare the town?

   He compares it to a living being.

2. The news of Kino's pearl spread quickly across town. What did each person think of when he heard it?

   Each person thinks of how he personally could benefit from the riches of the pearl.

3. What would Kino do with his riches?

   Kino would marry Juana, buy new clothes, a harpoon and a rifle, and send Coyotito to school.

4. Why does the doctor come? What does he do?

   The doctor comes because he, too, has heard that Kino has a great pearl. He wants to get some money from Kino, and we are led to believe that he has ideas of stealing the pearl for himself.

5. What bad thing happened to make Juana want to throw away the pearl?

   Someone comes to steal the pearl. Kino knifed him, but he got knocked over the head with something.

Chapter 4

1. In the description of the pearl buyers, what do we find out about the market in Kino's village?

   The market is fixed. The buyers get together and set prices to cheat the village men.

2. What happened when Kino went to sell his pearl?

   The pearl buyer told him it was a curiosity, not a valuable pearl. He offered Kino 1,000 pesos. When Kino disagreed, three other buyers were brought in; each one said it was of little value. It is made obvious to the reader that the buyers had arranged their prices earlier. Kino says he will go to the capitol instead of dealing with these buyers.

3. Juan Tomas says to Kino, "You have defied not the pearl buyers, but the whole structure, the whole way of life. I am afraid for you." What does he mean?
    No one of the village men had ever gone against the buyers. No one had "taken on city hall," so-to-speak. It was not Kino's place to try to do better. He was just a lowly village man; that was his station in life. Now, he was trying to improve his station and would have to have a major conflict in order to do so. Juan Tomas thinks this goes against the laws of nature and that bad things happen when you go against the laws of nature. As I heard it put once, "Little fish don't eat big fish."

4. Again at the end of the chapter, Juana wants to throw away the pearl because it is evil. What evil thing happened?
    Kino is attacked again. This time he is hurt worse than the first time.

Chapter 5
1. Where did Juana go early in the morning?
    Juana tried to sneak out with the pearl to throw it away.

2. What did Kino do when he figured out where she went?
    He went after her, took the pearl away, and (in the process) beat and kicked Juana.

3. What happened to Kino up the beach through the brushline on the path?
    He was attacked again. This time he was badly injured, and he killed a man. He thought he lost the pearl, but (ironically) Juana found it again in the path.

4. What happened to their hut while they were away?
    Someone had gone in searching for the pearl. It was a total wreck, then someone set fire to it.

5. Why did they leave the village?
    They left the village because Kino had killed a man. They did not think that, given Kino's recent upsetting of authority, anyone would believe the man was killed in self-defense.

Chapter 6
1. What "songs" does Kino hear on the first part of their journey?
    He hears the music of the pearl and the quiet melody of the family.

2. What made the music of the pearl become "sinister in his ears, . . . interwoven with the music of evil?"
    Kino looked at Coyotito's face. We assume that means he thought of the evil of the scorpion and his distrust of the doctor.

3. What happens to Coyotito?
    Coyotito cries. The tracker shoots towards the sound, towards the cave where Juana and Coyotito are hiding, and the shot hits and kills Coyotito.

4. What happens to the trackers?
    Kino kills the trackers.

5. What happens to Kino and Juana?
    They return to the village with their dead baby.

6. What do they do with the pearl?
    They throw it away.

7. What does the return of Kino and Juana and their throwing away the pearl mean symbolically?
    It means that Kino has given up his dream, his hope for a better future for himself and his family. He has lost in his conflicts with man and nature. It appears as though Juan Tomas was right.

MULTIPLE CHOICE STUDY GUIDE/QUIZ QUESTIONS - *The Pearl*

Chapter 1

1. Which of these does not happen in the first chapter?
    a. Kino and Juana wake up and prepare for the day.
    b. The neighbors walked into town with Kino and Juana.
    c. The scorpion strikes Coyotito.
    d. The doctor treats Coyotito's wound.

2. Why did the townspeople follow Kino?
    a. They were angry at his family.
    b. They were curious.
    c. They wanted to protect their homes.
    d. They were afraid of the scorpion.

3. Why did the doctor refuse to treat Coyotito?
    a. He thought of the Indians as animals.
    b. He didn't have the proper equipment.
    c. He had too many other patients to treat.
    d. He was ill himself.

4. How would you describe the doctor?
    a. Kind and considerate
    b. Stupid and lazy
    c. Materialistic and cold hearted
    d. Intelligent and energetic

5. Which of these is one of the conflicts in the story so far?
    a. Man vs. nature
    b. Heredity vs. environment
    c. Nature vs. society
    d. Man vs. religion

6. What is the Song of the Family about?
    a. A chronological history of Kino's family
    b. Peaceful existence and family harmony
    c. Family tragedy
    d. Kino and Juana's wedding song

7. What first brought the Song of Evil to Kino's mind?
    a. Kino and Juana have a fight.
    b. A terrible storm damages the town.
    c. The scorpion strikes the baby.
    d. Kino's brother is injured.

The Pearl Multiple Choice Study Guide Questions Page 2

Chapter 2

8. What theme does the first section about life in the Gulf waters show?
    a. Man's inhumanity to man
    b. The destruction of the environment
    c. Woman's role as caretaker
    d. The survival of the fittest

9. Of what is the canoe a symbol?
    a. The continuance of the family
    b. Great wealth
    c. Freedom
    d. Man's desire to explore

10. What is the main event of the chapter?
    a. Coyotito begins to heal
    b. Kino and Juana find the pearl.
    c. Juan Tomas fights with Kino.
    d. The scorpion scares the townspeople.

11. Everything goes well on the water. Of what is this symbolic?
    a. The value of tradition
    b. Trust in God
    c. Man's need to work hard
    d. Happiness and good in nature

12. What is the new Song?
    a. The Pearl That Might Be
    b. The Rescue of Coyotito
    c. The Luck of Kino and Juana
    d. The Loveliness of Nature

The Pearl Multiple Choice Study Guide Questions Page 3

Chapter 3

13. To what does Steinbeck compare the town?
    a. A violent storm
    b. A larger city
    c. A stubborn dog
    d. A living being

14. What did each person think of when he heard the news of the pearl?
    a. Its beauty
    b. Their personal benefit
    c. The prestige it would give the town
    d. Their happiness for Kino

15. Which would Kino not do with his riches?
    a. Move to the city
    b. Marry Juana in church
    c. Buy clothes and a harpoon
    d. Send Coyotito to school

16. Why does the doctor come to Kino's hut?
    a. He regrets that he did not treat Coyotito.
    b. The priest makes him come.
    c. He is thinking of stealing the pearl.
    d. He had left his instruments there.

17. What happened to make Juana want to throw away the pearl?
    a. The baby starts vomiting.
    b. Kino knifes a potential thief.
    c. The priest says having the pearl is a sin.
    d. The doctor says it is not worth anything.

The Pearl Multiple Choice Study Guide Questions Page 4

Chapter 4

18. What do we find out about the market in Kino's village?
    a. It always pays the highest rate.
    b. The buyers are very competitive.
    c. It is only open in the morning.
    d. The prices are fixed to cheat the villagers.

19. What did the buyers tell Kino about his pearl.
    a. It was not valuable
    b. He should go to the capital to sell it.
    c. It was the most beautiful pearl they had ever seen.
    d. They would pay fifty thousand pesos for it.

20. Juan Tomas says to Kino, "You have defied not the pearl buyers, but the whole structure, the whole way of life. I am afraid for you." What does he mean?
    a. The pearl buyers will not buy anymore pearls from Kino.
    b. It is not Kino's place to try and improve his life.
    c. It is against the law to refuse to sell a pearl to the buyers.
    d. Kino is becoming greedy and mean.

21. What happens to make Juana want to throw away the pearl.
    a. Coyotito tries to swallow the pearl.
    b. She thinks Kino will leave her and the baby.
    c. She thinks the pearl is causing a storm at sea.
    d. Kino is attacked again and is hurt even worse.

The Pearl Multiple Choice Study Guide Questions Page 5

Chapter 5

22. Where did Juana go early in the morning?
    a. To look for more pearls.
    b. To pay the doctor.
    c. To talk to the priest.
    d. To throw away the pearl.

23. What did Kino do when he figures out where she went?
    a. He went back to sleep
    b. He followed her and beat and kicked her.
    c. He went to his brother for help.
    d. He prayed for her.

24. What happened to Kino up the beach through the brushline on the path?
    a. He was attacked, he killed a man and lost the pearl.
    b. The buyers met him and offered him more money for the pearl.
    c. His brother came to warn him that robbers were after him.
    d. He tripped on a rock and broke his leg.

25. What happened to their hut while they were away?
    a. It was destroyed by a tidal wave.
    b. It was ransacked and burned.
    c. The neighbors kept watch so it would be safe.
    d. The priest came and blessed it.

26. Why did Juana and Kino leave the village?
    a. They heard of a buyer in the next town who was more honest.
    b. They went to look for a school for Coyotito.
    c. They were invited to meet the mayor of the city.
    d. They were afraid because Kino had killed a man.

The Pearl Multiple Choice Study Guide Questions Page 6

Chapter 6

27. What "songs" does Kino hear on the first part of their journey?
    a. The pearl and the family
    b. The water and the dark
    c. The family and the gods
    d. Evil and the pearl

28. What made the music of the pearl become "sinister in his ears...Interwoven with the music of evil?"
    a. Juana was disappointed that they had not been married in the church
    b. Kino could see someone following them
    c. Coyotito's feverish face reminded him of his distrust of the doctor
    d. They realized that wanting a rifle could be dangerous

29. What happens to Coyotito?
    a. He becomes delirious with fever
    b. He is shot by the tracker
    c. He is stung by another scorpion
    d. Juana must leave him behind because he is crying

30. What happens to the trackers?
    a. They get a reward for finding Kino.
    b. They are frightened because they think they hear coyotes.
    c. They are killed by Kino.
    d. They get lost in the mountains

31. What do Kino and Juana do?
    a. They continue on to the capital.
    b. They return to the village.
    c. They get married in the church.
    d. They have a funeral for Coyotito.

32. What do they do with the pearl?
    a. They donate it to the church.
    b. They bury it in Coyotito's grave.
    c. They sell it to the buyers for fifteen hundred pesos.
    d. They throw it back into the Gulf.

The Pearl Multiple Choice Study Guide Questions Page 7

33. What does their action with the pearl symbolize?
   a. Kino has lost in his conflicts with man and nature.
   b. Honor is more important than wealth.
   c. Juana wants Kino to give up diving for pearls.
   d. Man's will power is stronger than greed.

ANSWER KEY - MULTIPLE CHOICE STUDY/QUIZ QUESTIONS
The Pearl

Chapters 1 & 2	Chapter 3	Chapter 4 & 5	Chapter 6
1. D	13. D	18. D	27. A
2. B	14. B	19. A	28. C
3. A	15. A	20. B	29. B
4. C	16. C	21. D	30. C
5. A	17. B	22. D	31. B
6. B		23. B	32. D
7. C		24. A	33. A
8. D		25. B	
9. A		26. D	
10. B			
11. D			
12. A			

PREREADING VOCABULARY WORKSHEETS

VOCABULARY - *The Pearl*

<u>Chapter 1 & 2</u> Part I: Using Prior Knowledge and Contextual Clues

Below are the sentences in which the vocabulary words appear in the text. Read the sentence. Use any clues you can find in the sentence combined with your prior knowledge, and write what you think the underlined words mean on the lines provided.

1. The roosters had been crowing for some time, and the early pigs were already beginning their <u>ceaseless</u> turning of twigs and bits of wood to see whether anything to eat had been overlooked.

_____

2. On her hard bare feet she went to the hanging box where Coyotito slept, and she leaned over and said a little <u>reassuring</u> word.

_____

3. Kino watched with the detachment of God while a dusty ant <u>frantically</u> tried to escape the sand trap an ant lion had dug for him.

_____

4. They made a quick soft-footed procession into the center of the town, first Juana and Kino, and behind them Juan Tomas and Apolonia, her big stomach jiggling with the <u>strenuous</u> pace, then all the neighbors with the children trotting on the flanks.

_____

5. They knew his ignorance, his cruelty, his <u>avarice</u>, his appetites, his sins.

_____

6. She gathered some brown seaweed and made a flat, damp <u>poultice</u> of it, and this she applied to the baby's swollen shoulder...

_____

7. Above, the surface of the water was an <u>undulating</u> mirror of brightness...

_____

8. Kino moved cautiously so that the water would not be <u>obscured</u> with mud or sand.

_____

Vocabulary - *The Pearl* Chapter s 1-2 Continued

9. But in the song there was a secret little inner song, hardly <u>perceptible</u> but always there...

_____

10. It captured the light and refined it and gave it back in silver <u>incandescence</u>.

_____

Part II: Determining the Meaning

You have tried to figure out the meanings of the vocabulary words for Chapter 1 & 2. Now match the vocabulary words to their dictionary definitions. If there are words for which you cannot figure out the definition by contextual clues and by process of elimination, look them up in a dictionary.

___ 1. ceaseless　　　　　　A. covered over
___ 2. reassuring　　　　　　B. able to be detected by the senses
___ 3. frantically　　　　　　C. to cause to move in waves
___ 4. strenuous　　　　　　D. shining brilliantly
___ 5. avarice　　　　　　　E. wild with anger, pain, worry; frenzied
___ 6. poultice　　　　　　　F. greed for riches
___ 7. undulating　　　　　　G. a hot, moist mass of herbs
___ 8. obscured　　　　　　H. unceasing, continual
___ 9. perceptible　　　　　I. restoring to confidence, to assure anew
___10. incandescence　　　J. vigorous, active, arduous

Vocabulary - *The Pearl* Chapter 3

Part I: Using Prior Knowledge and Contextual Clues
Below are the sentences in which the vocabulary words appear in the text. Read the sentence. Use any clues you can find in the sentence combined with your prior knowledge, and write what you think the underlined words mean on the lines provided.

1. And when it was made plain who Kino was, the doctor grew stern and judicious at the same time.

_____

2. The essence of the pearl mixed with essence of men and a curious dark residue was precipitated.

_____

3. The essence of the pearl mixed with essence of men and a curious dark residue was precipitated.

_____

4. The essence of the pearl mixed with essence of men and a curious dark residue was precipitated.

_____

5. And the music of the pearl had merged with the music of the family so that one beautified the other.

_____

6. All of these things Kino saw in the lucent pearl and he said, "We will have new clothes."

_____

7. But Kino's face shone with prophecy.

_____

Vocabulary - *The Pearl* Chapter 3 Continued

8. If these things came to pass, they would recount how Kino looked and what he said and how his eyes shone, and they would say, "He was a man <u>transfigured</u>.

_____

9. His people brought him a little supper of chocolate and sweet cakes and fruit, and he stared at the food <u>discontentedly</u>.

_____

10. He was not good at <u>dissembling</u> and he was very well understood.

_____

Part II: Determining the Meaning

You have tried to figure out the meanings of the vocabulary words for Chapter 3. Now match the vocabulary words to their dictionary definitions. If there are words for which you cannot figure out the definition by contextual clues and by process of elimination, look them up in a dictionary.

___ 11. judicious   A. to shine
___ 12. essence   B. prediction of something
___ 13. residue   C. joined together
___ 14. precipitated   D. to change the figure or outward appearance
___ 15. merged   E. remainder
___ 16. lucent   F. wise and careful
___ 17. prophecy   G. with dissatisfaction
___ 18. transfigured   H. created
___ 19. discontentedly   I. inward nature of anything
___ 20. dissembling   J. concealing under a false appearance

Vocabulary - *The Pearl* Chapters 4 & 5

Part I: Using Prior Knowledge and Contextual Clues
  Below are the sentences in which the vocabulary words appear in the text. Read the sentence. Use any clues you can find in the sentence combined with your prior knowledge, and write what you think the underlined words mean on the lines provided.

1. For Kino and Juana, this was the morning of mornings of their lives <u>comparable</u> only to the day when the baby had been born.

_____

2. The neighbors peered around the doorway and a line of little boys <u>clambered</u> on the window bars and looked through.

_____

3. Now Kino's face was <u>perplexed</u> and worried.

_____

4. He felt the evil <u>coagulating</u> about him, and he was helpless to protect himself.

_____

5. He took it up, rolled it quickly between thumb and forefinger, and then cast it <u>contemptuously</u> back into the tray.

_____

6. Long after Juan Tomas had gone Kino sat <u>brooding</u> on his sleeping mat.

_____

7. A <u>lethargy</u> had settled on him, and a little gray hopelessness.

_____

8. And knowing this, she <u>abandoned</u> the past instantly.

_____

Vocabulary - *The Pearl* Chapters 4-5 Continued

9. Kino, hurrying toward his house, felt a surge of <u>exhilaration</u>.

_____

10. She, being the nearest woman relative, raised a formal <u>lament</u> for the dead of the family.

_____

Part II: Determining the Meaning
   You have tried to figure out the meanings of the vocabulary words for Chapter 4 & 5. Now match the vocabulary words to their dictionary definitions. If there are words for which you cannot figure out the definition by contextual clues and by process of elimination, look them up in a dictionary.

___ 21. comparable   A. to keep thinking about something in a troubled way
___ 22. clambered   B. given up, forsaken or deserted
___ 23. perplexed   C. to feel deep sorrow or express it by weeping
___ 24. coagulating   D. a condition of abnormal drowsiness
___ 25. contemptuously   E. a feeling of high spirits
___ 26. brooding   F. similar
___ 27. lethargy   G. becoming a soft semi-solid mass
___ 28. abandoned   H. climbed with effort or clumsily
___ 29. exhilaration   I. scornfully, disdainfully
___ 30. lament   J. troubled with uncertainty

Vocabulary - *The Pearl* Chapter 6

Part I: Using Prior Knowledge and Contextual Clues
　　Below are the sentences in which the vocabulary words appear in the text. Read the sentence. Use any clues you can find in the sentence combined with your prior knowledge, and write what you think the underlined words mean on the lines provided.

1. The wind cried and whisked in the brush and the family went on monotonously hour after hour.

_____

2. They were not near the Gulf now, and the air was dry and hot so that the brush cricked with heat and a good resinous smell came from it.

_____

3. But ahead were the naked granite mountains, rising out of erosion rubble and standing monolithic against the sky.

_____

4. High in the gray stone mountains, under a frowing peak, a little spring bubbled out of a rupture in the stone

_____

5. And the baby was weary and petulant and he cried softly until Juana gave him her breast, and then he gurgled and clucked against her.

_____

6. And the baby was weary and petulant and he cried softly until Juana gave him her breast, and then he gurgled and clucked against her.

_____

7. And then he looked apprehensively to the east,

_____

Vocabulary - *The Pearl* Chapter 6 Continued

8. His hands and feet <u>threshed</u> in the tangle of the wild grapevine, and he whimpered and gibbered as he tried to get up.

___

9. She was as <u>remote</u> and as removed as Heaven.

___

Part II: Determining the Meaning

You have tried to figure out the meanings of the vocabulary words for Chapter 6. Now match the vocabulary words to their dictionary definitions. If there are words for which you cannot figure out the definition by contextual clues and by process of elimination, look them up in a dictionary.

___ 31. monotonously   A. impatient or irritable
___ 32. resinous   B. anxious or fearful about the future
___ 33. monolithic   C. secluded or far off
___ 34. rupture   D. made of a single block of stone
___ 35. weary   E. beat about; moved about violently
___ 36. petulant   F. going in same tone without variation
___ 37. apprehensively   G. like resin, a semi-solid plant substance
___ 38. threshed   H. tired or worn out
___ 39. remote   I. crack; hole

ANSWER KEY - VOCABULARY
The Pearl

Chapters 1 & 2	Chapter 3	Chapters 4 & 5	Chapter 6
1. H	11. F	21. F	31. F
2. I	12. I	22. H	32. G
3. E	13. E	23. J	33. D
4. J	14. H	24. G	34. I
5. F	15. C	25. I	35. H
6. G	16. A	26. A	36. A
7. C	17. B	27. D	37. B
8. A	18. D	28. B	38. E
9. B	19. G	29. E	39. C
10. D	20. J	30. C	

DAILY LESSONS

LESSON ONE

Objectives
1. To introduce the *Pearl* unit
2. To distribute books and other related materials (study guides, reading assignments, etc.)
3. To preview the study questions for chapters 1-2
4. To familiarize students with the vocabulary for chapters 1-2

NOTE: Prior to this lesson you need to have prepared a bulletin board with background paper and the title "THE PEARL: DREAMS FOR THE FUTURE" and to have made the assignment for students to bring in pictures or objects (that can be attached to the bulletin board) that represent their hopes or dreams for the future.

Activity #1
    Tell students to get out the pictures or objects they have brought representing their hopes or dreams for the future. Have each student (one at a time) explain what his/her picture or object is or represents and then attach the picture or object to the bulletin board.

TRANSITION: Explain that a man in the story they are about to read finds a huge pearl and that the pearl represents his hopes and dreams for his future.

Activity #2
    Distribute the materials students will use in this unit. Explain in detail how students are to use these materials.

    Study Guides Students should read the study guide questions for each reading assignment prior to beginning the reading assignment to get a feeling for what events and ideas are important in the section they are about to read. After reading the section, students will (as a class or individually) answer the questions to review the important events and ideas from that section of the book. Students should keep the study guides as study materials for the unit test.

    Vocabulary Prior to reading a reading assignment, students will do vocabulary work related to the section of the book they are about to read. Following the completion of the reading of the book, there will be a vocabulary review of all the words used in the vocabulary assignments. Students should keep their vocabulary work as study materials for the unit test.

<u>Reading Assignment Sheet</u>   You need to fill in the reading assignment sheet to let students know by when their reading has to be completed. You can either write the assignment sheet up on a side blackboard or bulletin board and leave it there for students to see each day, or you can "ditto" copies for each student to have. In either case, you should advise students to become very familiar with the reading assignments so they know what is expected of them.

<u>Extra Activities Center</u>   The Extra Activities section of this unit contains suggestions for an extra library of related books and articles in your classroom as well as crossword and word search puzzles. Make an extra activities center in your room where you will keep these materials for students to use. (Bring the books and articles in from the library and keep several copies of the puzzles on hand.) Explain to students that these materials are available for students to use when they finish reading assignments or other class work early.

<u>Nonfiction Assignment Sheet</u>   Explain to students that they each are to read at least one non-fiction piece from the in-class library at some time during the unit. Students will fill out a nonfiction assignment sheet after completing the reading to help you evaluate their reading experiences and to help the students think about and evaluate their own reading experiences.

<u>Books</u>   Each school has its own rules and regulations regarding student use of school books. Advise students of the procedures that are normal for your school.

<u>Activity #3</u>
Preview the study questions and have students do the vocabulary work for Chapters 1-2 of *The Pearl*. If students do not finish this assignment during this class period, they should complete it prior to the next class meeting.

NONFICTION ASSIGNMENT SHEET
(To be completed after reading the required nonfiction article)

Name _____ Date _____

Title of Nonfiction Read _____

Written By _____ Publication Date _____

I. Factual Summary: Write a short summary of the piece you read.

II. Vocabulary
    1. With which vocabulary words in the piece did you encounter some degree of difficulty?

    2. How did you resolve your lack of understanding with these words?

III. Interpretation: What was the main point the author wanted you to get from reading his work?

IV. Criticism
    1. With which points of the piece did you agree or find easy to accept? Why?

    2. With which points of the piece did you disagree or find difficult to believe? Why?

V. Personal Response: What do you think about this piece? OR How does this piece influence your ideas?

LESSON TWO

Objectives
1. To read chapters 1-2
2. To give students practice reading orally
3. To evaluate students' oral reading

Activity

Have students read chapters 1-2 of *The Pearl* out loud in class. You probably know the best way to get readers with your class; pick students at random, ask for volunteers, or use whatever method works best for your group. If you have not yet completed an oral reading evaluation for your students this marking period, this would be a good opportunity to do so. A form is included with this unit for your convenience.

If students do not complete reading chapters 1-2 in class, they should do so prior to your next class meeting.

LESSON THREE

Objectives
1. To review the main events and ideas from chapters 1-2
2. To preview the study questions for chapter 3
3. To familiarize students with the vocabulary in chapter 3
4. To read chapter 3

Activity #1

Give students a few minutes to formulate answers for the study guide questions for chapters 1-2, and then discuss the answers to the questions in detail. Write the answers on the board or overhead transparency so students can have the correct answers for study purposes. Note: It is a good practice in public speaking and leadership skills for individual students to take charge of leading the discussions of the study questions. Perhaps a different student could go to the front of the class and lead the discussion each day that the study questions are discussed during this unit. Of course, the teacher should guide the discussion when appropriate and be sure to fill in any gaps the students leave.

Activity #2

Give students about fifteen minutes to preview the study questions for chapter 3 of *The Pearl* and to do the related vocabulary work.

Activity #3

Tell students to read chapter 3 of *The Pearl* prior to your next class period. If there is time remaining in this period, students may begin reading silently.

ORAL READING EVALUATION - *The Pearl*

Name _____ Class _____ Date _____

SKILL	EXCELLENT	GOOD	AVERAGE	FAIR	POOR
Fluency	5	4	3	2	1
Clarity	5	4	3	2	1
Audibility	5	4	3	2	1
Pronunciation	5	4	3	2	1
_____	5	4	3	2	1
_____	5	4	3	2	1

Total _____ Grade _____

Comments:

LESSON FOUR

Objectives
1. To review the main ideas and events from Chapter 3
2. To give students the opportunity to express their own personal ideas in writing
3. To give the teacher the opportunity to evaluate students' writing skills
4. To help students identify with Kino and what the pearl meant to him and his family
5. To complete the prereading work for chapters 4-5

Activity #1
Give students a few minutes to formulate answers for the study guide questions for chapter 3, and then discuss the answers to the questions in detail. Write the answers on the board or overhead transparency so students can have the correct answers for study purposes.

Activity #2
Distribute Writing Assignment #1. Discuss the directions in detail and give students ample time to complete the assignment.

Activity #3
Tell students that prior to your next class period they should complete the prereading work (reviewing the study questions and completing the vocabulary worksheet) for chapters 4-5.

LESSON FIVE

Objectives
1. To complete the oral reading evaluations
2. To read chapters 4-5

Activity
Have students read chapters 4 and 5 orally in class. If you have not yet completed the oral reading evaluations, do so in this class period if at all possible.

WRITING ASSIGNMENT #1 - *The Pearl*

PROMPT

Finding the pearl was a monumental occasion for Kino and his family. With the money the pearl would bring, all Kino's dreams for the future could be fulfilled.

It's not likely that any of us will ever discover a pearl. The one thing in our society that could possibly be the equivalent would be for us to win the lottery or a sweepstakes. The chances of winning such games are probably no better than Kino's chances of finding a beautiful pearl. Bearing that in mind, you can perhaps begin to understand how Kino must have felt when he found the pearl.

Your assignment is to write a composition in which you tell what you would do if you were to win the lottery or a sweepstakes and suddenly become rich like Kino did upon finding the pearl. How would you fulfill your hopes and dreams for the future?

PREWRITING

Stop and think for a minute. What things in life are most important to you? What *are* your hopes and dreams for the future? Make a few notes about each of your ideas. Next to each of your notes about your hopes and dreams, write down how your newly acquired money could help you make your dreams come true.

DRAFTING

Write an introductory paragraph in which you introduce the ideas that you have suddenly become rich and that you think this money will help you fulfill your hopes and dreams.

In the body of your paper, write a paragraph for each of your hopes and/or dreams. Within each paragraph, explain what your hope/dream is and how you will use your money to help fulfill that hope/dream.

Write a concluding paragraph in which you sum up your ideas and bring your composition to a close.

PROMPT

When you finish the rough draft of your paper, ask a student who sits near you to read it. After reading your rough draft, he/she should tell you what he/she liked best about your work, which parts were difficult to understand, and ways in which your work could be improved. Reread your paper considering your critic's comments, and make the corrections you think are necessary.

PROOFREADING

Do a final proofreading of your paper double-checking your grammar, spelling, organization, and the clarity of your ideas.

LESSON SIX

Objectives
1. To review the main ideas of chapters 4-5
2. To preview the study questions for chapter 6
3. To read chapter 6

Activity #1
Ask students to get out their books and some paper (not their study guides). Tell students to write down ten questions (and answers) which cover the main events and ideas in chapter 6.

Discuss the students questions and answers orally, making a list of the questions with brief responses on the board. Put a star next to the students' questions and answers that are essentially the same as the study guide questions. (Be sure that all the study guide questions are answered.)

Activity #2
Tell students to preview the study questions and do the vocabulary work for chapter 6.

Activity #3
Tell students that they should read chapter 6 prior to your next class meeting. If they have time after completing Activity #2, they may use the remainder of this class period to begin their reading.

LESSON SEVEN

Objectives
1. To review the main ideas and events from chapter 6
2. To discuss *The Pearl* on interpretive and critical levels

Activity #1
Take a few minutes at the beginning of the period to review the study questions for chapter 6.

Activity #2
Choose the questions from the Extra Discussion Questions/Writing Assignments which seem most appropriate for your students. A class discussion of these questions is most effective if students have been given the opportunity to formulate answers to the questions prior to the discussion. To this end, you may either have all the students formulate answers to all the questions, divide your class into groups and assign one or more questions to each group, or you could assign one question to each student in your class. The option you choose will make a difference in the amount of class time needed for this activity.

Activity #3
After students have had ample time to formulate answers to the questions, begin your class discussion of the questions and the ideas presented by the questions. Be sure students take notes during the discussion so they have information to study for the unit test.

LESSON EIGHT

Objective
To review all of the vocabulary work done in this unit

Activity
Choose one (or more) of the vocabulary review activities listed below and spend your class period as directed in the activity. Some of the materials for these review activities are located in the Vocabulary Resource section in this unit.

EXTRA WRITING ASSIGNMENTS/DISCUSSION QUESTIONS - *The Pearl*

Interpretation
1. What point of view does Steinbeck use for *The Pearl*? How does this contribute to our understanding of the themes in the story?
2. Write a list of the main events in *The Pearl*.
3. Is the story of *The Pearl* believable? Why or why not?
4. What are the main settings throughout the story? What do they add to the story?
5. Are the characters in *The Pearl* stereotypes? If so, why are stereotypes used? If not, explain how they merit individuality?
6. What are the main conflicts in the story, and how are they resolved?

Critical
7. Explain how *The Pearl* is a parable.
8. Are Kino's actions believably motivated? Explain why or why not.
9. What is the role of the trackers in the story? Why were they included?
10. Evaluate John Steinbeck's style of writing. How does it contribute to the value of the novel?
11. Compare and contrast Juana and Kino.
12. Compare and contrast the doctor, the priest, and the buyers.
13. Explain how John Steinbeck uses the buyers to develop the idea that "you can't fight city hall."
14. Explain Coyotito's role in the novel. Why was he included?

Critical/Personal Response
15. If this story were told in the first person narrative by Juana, how would the story and its effect have changed?
16. Who is responsible for the townspeople's situation with the buyers? Explain why.
17. *The Pearl* is a short novel. Could anything have been gained by including more scenes from the time before or after the events of the story? If so, what could have been added and for what purpose? If not, explain why not.
18. Was Kino greedy? Explain why or why not.
19. Who is responsible for Coyotito's death? Justify your answer.
20. What does Kino's defeat signify? Do you agree or disagree?

Personal Response
21. Did you enjoy reading *The Pearl*? Why or why not?
22. Suppose Kino would tell you about the events of this story a few years later. What do you think he would say?
23. Define a doctor's responsibility to society. Is there a limit to what society has a right to demand of a doctor?

VOCABULARY REVIEW ACTIVITIES

1. Divide your class into two teams and have an old-fashioned spelling or definition bee.

2. Give each of your students (or students in groups of two, three or four) a *The Pearl* Vocabulary Word Search Puzzle. The person (group) to find all of the vocabulary words in the puzzle first wins.

3. Give students a *The Pearl* Vocabulary Word Search Puzzle without the word list. The person or group to find the most vocabulary words in the puzzle wins.

4. Use a *The Pearl* Vocabulary Crossword Puzzle. Put the puzzle onto a transparency on the overhead projector (so everyone can see it), and do the puzzle together as a class.

5. Give students a *The Pearl* Vocabulary Matching Worksheet to do.

6. Divide your class into two teams. Use the *Pearl* vocabulary words with their letters jumbled as a word list. Student 1 from Team A faces off against Student 1 from Team B. You write the first jumbled word on the board. The first student (1A or 1B) to unscramble the word wins the chance for his/her team to score points. If 1A wins the jumble, go to student 2A and give him/her a definition. He/she must give you the correct spelling of the vocabulary word which fits that definition. If he/she does, Team A scores a point, and you give student 3A a definition for which you expect a correctly spelled matching vocabulary word. Continue giving Team A definitions until some team member makes an incorrect response. An incorrect response sends the game back to the jumbled-word face off, this time with students 2A and 2B. Instead of repeating giving definitions to the first few students of each team, continue with the student after the one who gave the last incorrect response on the team. For example, if Team B wins the jumbled-word face-off, and student 5B gave the last incorrect answer for Team B, you would start this round of definition questions with student 6B, and so on. The team with the most points wins!

7. Have students write a story in which they correctly use as many vocabulary words as possible. Have students read their compositions orally! Post the most original compositions on your bulletin board.

LESSON NINE

Objectives
    1. To give students the opportunity to practice writing to persuade
    2. To give the teacher the opportunity to evaluate students' writing skills
    3. To review the events of the story
    4. To further study the character of Juana

Activity
    Distribute Writing Assignment #2. Discuss the directions in detail and then give students ample time to complete the assignment.

    Follow-Up: After you have graded the assignments, have a writing conference with the students. (This unit schedules one in Lesson Twelve.) After the writing conference, allow students to revise their papers using your suggestions and corrections. Give them about three days from the date they receive their papers to complete the revision. I suggest grading the revisions on an A-C-E scale (all revisions well-done, some revisions made, few or no revisions made). This will speed your grading time and still give some credit for the students' efforts.

WRITING ASSIGNMENT #2 - *The Pearl*

PROMPT
You are Juana, hiding with Kino and Coyotito in the cave in the mountains. The trackers have not yet arrived. What would you say to convince Kino to go home and throw the pearl back into the water?

PREWRITING
Make a list of the bad things that have happened since Kino found the pearl. You are Juana. Why do you want Kino to get rid of the pearl? Make a list of your reasons. You are still Juana, but look at the situation from Kino's point of view. If you were Kino, what things would motivate you to throw that pearl away? Make a list of those things.

DRAFTING
Write an introductory paragraph in which you bring up the subject of throwing away the pearl to Kino.

In the body of your composition, write one paragraph for each of the reasons you want Kino to get rid of the pearl. Also write one paragraph for each of the things that will motivate Kino to get rid of the pearl.

Write a concluding paragraph in which you summarize your arguments and make your final appeal.

PROMPT
When you finish the rough draft of your paper, ask a student who sits near you to read it. After reading your rough draft, he/she should tell you what he/she liked best about your work, which parts were difficult to understand, and ways in which your work could be improved. Reread your paper considering your critic's comments, and make the corrections you think are necessary.

PROOFREADING
Do a final proofreading of your paper double-checking your grammar, spelling, organization, and the clarity of your ideas.

LESSON TEN

Objectives
1. To study the novel more closely through all six chapters
2. To give students the opportunity to practice their personal interaction skills in a small group setting
3. To give students the opportunity to practice their public speaking skills as they report their small group findings

NOTE: These activities may take more than one class period depending on the ability level of your students and the depth in which you discuss each of these topics.

Activity #1

Divide the class into six groups. Each group should be assigned one of the following topics: light and dark images, symbols, roles of men and women, good vs. evil, songs, and animal imagery. Students within the group will each take one chapter of *The Pearl* and find all the references to their group's topic in that chapter. (If the groups have more than six people, have more than one student work on the same chapter. If the groups have less than six people, the group members will have to cover more than one chapter.) Students should jot down their findings. When the individuals are done with their research, group members should get together to discuss their findings. Based on their research, they should try to draw some conclusions about the topic.

Activity #2

The groups will each report their findings and conclusions to the whole class. Each student will give his findings, and one group member will give the group's conclusions.

The teacher or a student should write down on the board or overhead all of the findings and conclusions. If you have enough room, a chart format would be helpful for students' study purposes. (Students should all take notes from the board for later study.)

LESSON ELEVEN

Objectives
1. To check students understanding of the meanings of the songs in the story
2. To have students describe the intangible feelings implied by the songs, in concrete words

Activity

With student input, make a list of all the "songs" in *The Pearl*. Write the list on the chalkboard. Explain to students that their assignment is to write the lyrics to each of the songs on the list. In choosing the words to use, students should consider the rhythm of the words. Is the rhythm compatible with the meaning of the song? Students should also choose their words carefully to express the meaning of the song.

LESSON TWELVE

Objectives
1. To give students the opportunity to explore nonfiction topics related to the story
2. To give students the opportunity to use the library
3. To broaden students' knowledge of our world
4. To hold writing conferences with individual students

Activity #1
Take students to the library. Explain to them that this is their opportunity to complete the nonfiction reading assignment which accompanies this unit. Students are to find nonfiction books or articles in some way relating to *The Pearl*. Students are to use this time to find nonfiction materials that interest them and to begin reading. Remind students to complete the Nonfiction Assignment Sheet after they have done their reading.

Remind students that they will be giving a little oral report about their nonfiction reading in Lesson Fourteen. (Give students a day and a date.)

Suggested Topics (Feel free to add to this list.)

Diving
Gemstone industry
Responsibilities of doctors
Stories about people who have "fought city hall"
Careers in medicine, the gemstone industry, detective work, or the seafood industry
Boating
Stories about what people who have won lotteries or sweepstakes have done with
    their winnings
Scorpions
Tracking
Caves and cave exploration

Activity #2
While students are finding materials and reading, call individual students over to a private area where you can hold writing conferences. An evaluation form is included with this unit for your convenience.

WRITING EVALUATION FORM - *The Pearl*

Name _____ Date _____

Writing Assignment #1 for the *Pearl* unit   Grade _____

Grammar: correct   errors noted on paper

Spelling: correct   errors noted on paper

Punctuation: correct   errors noted on paper

Legibility: excellent   good   fair   poor

Strengths:

Weaknesses:

Comments/Suggestions:

LESSON THIRTEEN

Objectives
1. To give students the opportunity to practice writing to inform
2. To give the teacher a chance to evaluate students' individual writing
3. To help students gather their thoughts for their oral presentations

Activity

Distribute Writing Assignment #3. Discuss the directions orally in detail. Allow the remaining class time for students to complete the activity.

Follow-Up: Follow up as in Writing Assignment 2, allowing students to correct their errors and turn in the revision for credit. A good time for your next writing conferences would be the day following the unit test.

WRITING ASSIGNMENT #3 - *The Pearl*

PROMPT

You have read at least one article of nonfiction relating to *The Pearl*. Now you are to write a composition in which you summarize your article(s). This is to help you review the information as well as to help prepare you for your oral presentation.

PREWRITING

Your reading has been done, and you probably have some notes on paper sitting in front of you. Look at your notes and begin to organize them. Arrange the notes in an order that makes sense: chronological order (order of time that the events happen) is often appropriate.

DRAFTING

Start with a paragraph in which you introduce your topic. In the body of your paper write your summary. Finally, write a paragraph in which you give your opinions about your topic (tell whether you agree or disagree with the article, for example).

PROMPT

When you finish the rough draft of your paper, ask a student who sits near you to read it. After reading your rough draft, he/she should tell you what he/she liked best about your work, which parts were difficult to understand, and ways in which your work could be improved. Reread your paper considering your critic's comments, and make the corrections you think are necessary.

PROOFREADING

Do a final proofreading of your paper double-checking your grammar, spelling, organization, and the clarity of your ideas.

LESSON FOURTEEN

Objectives
    1. To widen the breadth of students' knowledge about the topics discussed or touched upon in *The Pearl*
    2. To check students' nonfiction reading assignments

Activity
    Ask each student to give a brief oral report about the nonfiction work he/she read for the nonfiction reading assignment. Your criteria for evaluating this report will vary depending on the level of your students. You may wish for students to give a complete report without using notes of any kind, or you may want students to read directly from a written report, or you may want to do something in between these two extremes. Just make students aware of your criteria in ample time for them to prepare their reports.

    Start with one student's report. After that, ask if anyone else in the class has read on a topic related to the first student's report. If no one has, choose another student at random. After each report, be sure to ask if anyone has a report related to the one just completed. That will help keep a continuity during the discussion of the reports.

LESSON FIFTEEN

Objective
    To review the main ideas presented in *The Pearl*

Activity #1
    Choose one of the review games/activities included in the packet and spend your class period as outlined there. Some materials for these activities are located in the Extra Activities Packet section of this unit.

Activity #2
    Remind students that the Unit Test will be in the next class meeting. Stress the review of the Study Guides and their class notes as a last minute, brush-up review for homework.

REVIEW GAMES/ACTIVITIES - *The Pearl*

1. Ask the class to make up a unit test for *The Pearl*. The test should have 4 sections: matching, true/false, short answer, and essay. Students may use 1/2 period to make the test and then swap papers and use the other 1/2 class period to take a test a classmate has devised. (open book) You may want to use the unit test included in this packet or take questions from the students' unit tests to formulate your own test.

2. Take 1/2 period for students to make up true and false questions (including the answers). Collect the papers and divide the class into two teams. Draw a big tic-tac-toe board on the chalk board. Make one team X and one team O. Ask questions to each side, giving each student one turn. If the question is answered correctly, that students' team's letter (X or O) is placed in the box. If the answer is incorrect, no mark is placed in the box. The object is to get three marks in a row like tic-tac-toe. You may want to keep track of the number of games won for each team.

3. Take 1/2 period for students to make up questions (true/false and short answer). Collect the questions. Divide the class into two teams. You'll alternate asking questions to individual members of teams A & B (like in a spelling bee). The question keeps going from A to B until it is correctly answered, then a new question is asked. A correct answer does not allow the team to get another question. Correct answers are +2 points; incorrect answers are -1 point.

4. Have students pair up and quiz each other from their study guides and class notes.

5. Give students a *The Pearl* crossword puzzle to complete.

6. Divide your class into two teams. Use the *Pearl* crossword words with their letters jumbled as a word list. Student 1 from Team A faces off against Student 1 from Team B. You write the first jumbled word on the board. The first student (1A or 1B) to unscramble the word wins the chance for his/her team to score points. If 1A wins the jumble, go to student 2A and give him/her a clue. He/she must give you the correct word which matches that clue. If he/she does, Team A scores a point, and you give student 3A a clue for which you expect another correct response. Continue giving Team A clues until some team member makes an incorrect response. An incorrect response sends the game back to the jumbled-word face off, this time with students 2A and 2B. Instead of repeating giving clues to the first few students of each team, continue with the student after the one who gave the last incorrect response on the team. For example, if Team B wins the jumbled-word face-off, and student 5B gave the last incorrect answer for Team B, you would start this round of clue questions with student 6B, and so on. The team with the most points wins!

UNIT TESTS

SHORT ANSWER UNIT TEST 1 - *The Pearl*

I. IDENTIFY

1. Kino

2. Juana

3. Coyotito

4. Doctor

5. Priest

6. Buyers

7. Trackers

8. Juan Tomas

9. Apolonia

10. Steinbeck

II. FOR WHAT DID THESE SYMBOLS/IMAGES STAND? (MATCHING)

____ 1. The pearl   A. Good;Tradition

____ 2. The canoe   B. Evil;Corruption

____ 3. The hut   C. Freedom/Hope

____ 4. The scorpion

____ 5. Coyotito's education

____ 6. The Song of the Family

____ 7. The Song of Evil

____ 8. The Song of the Pearl That Might Be

The Pearl Short Answer Unit Test 1 Page 2

III. SHORT ANSWER

1. What happened to Coyotito in the first chapter?

2. What happened when Kino went to sell his pearl?

3. Juan Tomas said to Kino, "You have defied not the pearl buyers, but the whole structure, the whole way of life. I am afraid for you." Explain.

4. Why did Kino, Juana and Coyotito leave the village?

5. In the end, what happens to:

   a. Kino and Juana

   b. Coyotito

   c. The Pearl

The Pearl Short Answer Unit Test 1 Page 3

IV. ESSAY

    What is the point of The Pearl? What message did Steinbeck want to convey?

IV. VOCABULARY

    Listen to the vocabulary words and write them down. Go back later and fill in the correct definition for each word.

1.

2.

3.

4.

5.

6.

7.

8.

9.

10.

SHORT ANSWER UNIT TEST 2 - *The Pearl*

I. MATCHING

___ 1. Kino   A. Was stung by a scorpion

___ 2. Juana   B. Accidentally killed Coyotito

___ 3. Coyotito   C. Tried to cheat Kino

___ 4. Doctor   D. Kino's brother

___ 5. Priest   E. He found the Pearl

___ 6. Buyers   F. Author

___ 7. Trackers   G. Juan Tomas's wife

___ 8. Juan Tomas   H. Refused to treat Coyotito until he heard about the pearl

___ 9. Apolonia   I. Kino's wife

___ 10. Steinbeck   J. Wanted Kino's wealth for the church

___ 11. Pearl   K. Good; tradition

___ 12. Canoe   L. Evil; corruption

___ 13. Scorpion   M. Freedom; hope

___ 14. Hut

___ 15. Song of the Family

___ 16. Song of the Pearl

Pearl Short Answer Unit Test 2 Page 2

II. SHORT ANSWER

1. Why did Steinbeck include the first section about the life in the Gulf waters?

2. Is it coincidence that everything goes well on the water, or is Steinbeck trying to show something?

3. The news of Kino's pearl spread quickly across town. What did each person think of when he heard it?

4. What would Kino do with his riches?

5. In the description of the pearl buyers, what do we find out about the market in Kino's village?

6. Juan Tomas says to Kino, "You have defied not the pearl buyers, but the whole structure, the whole way of life. I am afraid for you." What does he mean?

7. Why did Kino and his family leave the village?

8. What does the return of Kino and Juana and their throwing away the pearl mean symbolically?

Pearl Short Answer Unit Test 2 Page 3

III. ESSAY

Using specific examples from the text, explain how *The Pearl* is a story of good versus evil.

IV. VOCABULARY

Listen to the vocabulary words and write them down. Go back later and fill in the correct definition for each word.

1.
2.
3.
4.
5.
6.
7.
8.
9.
10.

KEY: SHORT ANSWER UNIT TESTS - *The Pearl*

The short answer questions are taken directly from the study guides.
If you need to look up the answers, you will find them in the study guide section.

Answers to the composition questions will vary depending on your
class discussions and the level of your students.

For the vocabulary section of the test, choose ten of the
words from the vocabulary lists to read orally for your students.

The answers to the matching section of the test are below.

Answers to the matching section of the Advanced Short Answer Unit Test
are the same as for Short Answer Unit Test #2.

<u>Test #1</u>
1. C
2. A
3. A
4. B
5. C
6. A
7. B
8. C

<u>Test #2</u>
1. E
2. I
3. A
4. H
5. J
6. C
7. B
8. D
9. G
10. F
11. M
12. K
13. L
14. K
15. K
16. M

ADVANCED SHORT ANSWER UNIT TEST - *The Pearl*

I. MATCHING

___ 1. Kino   A. Was stung by a scorpion

___ 2. Juana   B. Accidentally killed Coyotito

___ 3. Coyotito   C. Tried to cheat Kino

___ 4. Doctor   D. Kino's brother

___ 5. Priest   E. He found the Pearl

___ 6. Buyers   F. Author

___ 7. Trackers   G. Juan Tomas's wife

___ 8. Juan Tomas   H. Refused to treat Coyotito until he heard about the pearl

___ 9. Apolonia   I. Kino's wife

___ 10. Steinbeck   J. Wanted Kino's wealth for the church

___ 11. Pearl   K. Good; tradition

___ 12. Canoe   L. Evil; corruption

___ 13. Scorpion   M. Freedom; hope

___ 14. Hut

___ 15. Song of the Family

___ 16. Song of the Pearl

Pearl Advanced Short Answer Unit Test Page 2

II. ESSAY
Write at least a good paragraph to answer each of the following:

1. What are the main conflicts in the story, and how are they resolved?

2. Explain how *The Pearl* is a parable.

3. What is the role of the trackers in the story? Why were they included?

4. Compare and contrast Juana and Kino.

5. Explain how Steinbeck uses the buyers to develop the idea that "you can't fight city hall."

Pearl Advanced Short Answer Unit Test Page 3

6. Explain Coyotito's role in the novel. Why was he included?

7. Who is responsible for Coyotito's death? Justify your answer.

8. What does Kino's defeat signify? Do you agree or disagree?

9. Symbolism is important in *The Pearl*. Choose any four symbols used in the story. Explain how each is used and what each represents.

10. Why did Kino throw the pearl away?

Pearl Advanced Short Answer Unit Test Page 4

IV. VOCABULARY

Listen to the vocabulary words and write them down. Go back later and write a composition in which you use all of the words. The composition must relate in some way to *The Pearl*.

MULTIPLE CHOICE UNIT TEST 1 - *The Pearl*

I. MATCHING

___ 1. Kino   A. Kino's brother

___ 2. Juana   B. Author

___ 3. Coyotito   C. Juan Tomas's wife

___ 4. Doctor   D. Was stung by a scorpion

___ 5. Priest   E. Kino's wife

___ 6. Buyers   F. Accidentally killed Coyotito

___ 7. Trackers   G. Tried to cheat Kino

___ 8. Juan Tomas   H. Wanted Kino's wealth for the church

___ 9. Apolonia   I. He found the Pearl

___ 10. Steinbeck   J. Refused to treat Coyotito until he heard about the pearl

___ 11. Pearl   K. Freedom; hope

___ 12. Canoe   L. Good; tradition

___ 13. Scorpion   M. Evil; corruption

___ 14. Hut

___ 15. Song of the Family

___ 16. Song of the Pearl

The Pearl Multiple Choice Unit Test 1 Page 2

II. MULTIPLE CHOICE

1. Why did the doctor refuse to treat Coyotito?
    a. He thought of the Indians as animals.
    b. He didn't have the proper equipment.
    c. He had too many other patients to treat.
    d. He was ill himself.

2. What theme does the first section about life in the Gulf waters show?
    a. Man's inhumanity to man
    b. The destruction of the environment
    c. Woman's role as caretaker
    d. The survival of the fittest

3. Everything goes well on the water. Of what is this symbolic?
    a. The value of tradition
    b. Trust in God
    c. Man's need to work hard
    d. Happiness and good in nature

4. Which would Kino not do with his riches?
    a. Move to the city
    b. Marry Juana in church
    c. Buy clothes and a harpoon
    d. Send Coyotito to school

5. What do we find out about the market in Kino's village?
    a. It always pays the highest rate.
    b. The buyers are very competitive.
    c. It is only open in the morning.
    d. The prices are fixed to cheat the villagers.

6. Juan Tomas says to Kino, "You have defied not the pearl buyers, but the whole structure, the whole way of life. I am afraid for you." What does he mean?
    a. The pearl buyers will not buy any more pearls from Kino.
    b. It is not Kino's place to try and improve his life.
    c. It is against the law to refuse to sell a pearl to the buyers.
    d. Kino is becoming greedy and mean.

The Pearl Multiple Choice Unit Test 1 Page 3

7. What happened to Kino up the beach through the brushline on the path?
    a. He was attacked, he killed a man and lost the pearl.
    b. The buyers met him and offered him more money for the pearl.
    c. His brother came to warn him that robbers were after him.
    d. He tripped on a rock and broke his leg.

8. Why did Juana and Kino leave the village?
    a. They heard of a buyer in the next town who was more honest.
    b. They went to look for a school for Coyotito.
    c. They were invited to meet the mayor of the city.
    d. They were afraid because Kino had killed a man.

9. What made the music of the pearl become "sinister in his ears...Interwoven with the music of evil?"
    a. Juana was disappointed that they had not been married in the church.
    b. Kino could see someone following them.
    c. Coyotito's feverish face reminded him of his distrust of the doctor.
    d. They realized that wanting a rifle could be dangerous.

10. What do they do with the pearl?
    a. They donate it to the church.
    b. They bury it in Coyotito's grave.
    c. They sell it to the buyers for fifteen hundred pesos.
    d. They throw it back into the Gulf.

11. What does their action with the pearl symbolize?
    a. Kino has lost in his conflicts with man and nature.
    b. Honor is more important than wealth.
    c. Juana wants Kino to give up diving for pearls.
    d. Man's will power is stronger than greed.

12. What do the buyers and the doctor represent?
    a. The importance of capitalism
    b. Man's corruption
    c. An uncaring natural universe
    d. The sanctity of man's values

The Pearl Multiple Choice Unit Test 1 Page 4

13. Which of the following was NOT a main conflict in the story?
    a. Man versus man
    b. Man versus nature
    c. Man versus society
    d. Man versus idealism

14. Which of the following was NOT one of the "songs" in the story?
    a. Song of the Family
    b. Song of Lamenting
    c. Song of the Pearl
    d. Song of Evil

The Pearl Multiple Choice Unit Test 1 Page 5

IV. VOCABULARY- Match the correct definitions to the words.

___ 1. Transfigured   a. distant or secluded

___ 2. Lucent   b. becoming a soft semi-solid mass

___ 3. Remote   c. a condition of abnormal drowsiness

___ 4. Ceaseless   d. prediction

___ 5. Petulant   e. vigorous

___ 6. Prophecy   f. a hot moist mass of herbs

___ 7. Monolithic   g. changed in outward appearance

___ 8. Rupture   h. crack; hole

___ 9. Avarice   i. impatient or irritable

___ 10. Poultice   j. made of a single block of stone

___ 11. Comparable   k. shining, giving off light

___ 12. Lament   l. a sold or semi-sold substance from a plant

___ 13. Contemptuously   m. unceasing, continual

___ 14. Coagulating   n. similar

___ 15. Undulating   o. too great a desire to have wealth and riches

___ 16. Judicious   p. wise and careful

___ 17. Strenuous   q. scornfully or disdainfully

___ 18. Resinous   r. expression of deep sorrow by weeping or wailing

___ 19. Lethargy   s. a feeling of high spirits

___ 20. Exhilaration   t. to cause to move in waves

MULTIPLE CHOICE UNIT TEST 2 - *The Pearl*

I. MATCHING

___ 1. Kino   A. Juan Tomas's wife

___ 2. Juana   B. Kino's wife

___ 3. Coyotito   C. Accidentally killed Coyotito

___ 4. Doctor   D. Author

___ 5. Priest   E. Was stung by a scorpion

___ 6. Buyers   F. Tried to cheat Kino

___ 7. Trackers   G. Kino's brother

___ 8. Juan Tomas   H. Refused to treat Coyotito until he heard about the pearl

___ 9. Apolonia   I. Wanted Kino's wealth for the church

___ 10. Steinbeck   J. He found the Pearl

___ 11. Pearl   K. Evil; corruption

___ 12. Canoe   L. Freedom; hope

___ 13. Scorpion   M. Good; tradition

___ 14. Hut

___ 15. Song of the Family

___ 16. Song of the Pearl

The Pearl Multiple Choice Unit Test 2 Page 2

II. MULTIPLE CHOICE

1. Why did the doctor refuse to treat Coyotito?
    a. He had too many other patients to treat.
    b. He didn't have the proper equipment.
    c. He thought of the Indians as animals.
    d. He was ill himself.

2. What theme does the first section about life in the Gulf waters show?
    a. Woman's role as caretaker
    b. The destruction of the environment
    c. Man's inhumanity to man
    d. The survival of the fittest

3. Everything goes well on the water. Of what is this symbolic?
    a. Happiness and good in nature
    b. Trust in God
    c. Man's need to work hard
    d. The value of tradition

4. Which would Kino not do with his riches?
    a. Marry Juana in church
    b. Move to the city
    c. Buy clothes and a harpoon
    d. Send Coyotito to school

5. What do we find out about the market in Kino's village?
    a. It always pays the highest rate.
    b. The buyers are very competitive.
    c. The prices are fixed to cheat the villagers.
    d. It is only open in the morning.

6. Juan Tomas says to Kino, "You have defied not the pearl buyers, but the whole structure, the whole way of life. I am afraid for you." What does he mean?
    a. It is not Kino's place to try to improve his life.
    b. The pearl buyers will not buy anymore pearls from Kino.
    c. It is against the law to refuse to sell a pearl to the buyers.
    d. Kino is becoming greedy and mean.

The Pearl Multiple Choice Unit Test 2 Page 3

7. What happened to Kino up the beach through the brushline on the path?
    a. He tripped on a rock and broke his leg.
    b. The buyers met him and offered him more money for the pearl.
    c. His brother came to warn him that robbers were after him.
    d. He was attacked, he killed a man and lost the pearl.

8. Why did Juana and Kino leave the village?
    a. They heard of a buyer in the next town who was more honest.
    b. They went to look for a school for Coyotito.
    c. They were afraid because Kino had killed a man.
    d. They were invited to meet the mayor of the city.

9. What made the music of the pearl become "sinister in his ears...Interwoven with the music of evil?"
    a. Juana was disappointed that they had not been married in the church
    b. Coyotito's feverish face reminded him of his distrust of the doctor
    c. Kino could see someone following them
    d. They realized that wanting a rifle could be dangerous

10. What do they do with the pearl?
    a. They donate it to the church.
    b. They throw it back into the Gulf.
    c. They sell it to the buyers for fifteen hundred pesos.
    d. They bury it in Coyotito's grave.

11. What does their action with the pearl symbolize?
    a. Honor is more important than wealth.
    b. Kino has lost in his conflicts with man and nature.
    c. Juana wants Kino to give up diving for pearls.
    d. Man's will power is stronger than greed.

12. What do the buyers and the doctor represent?
    a. The importance of capitalism
    b. An uncaring natural universe
    c. Man's corruption
    d. The sanctity of man's values

The Pearl Multiple Choice Unit Test 2 Page 4

13. Which of the following was NOT a main conflict in the story?
    a. Man versus man
    b. Man versus idealism
    c. Man versus society
    d. Man versus nature

14. Which of the following was NOT one of the "songs" in the story?
    a. Song of the Family
    b. Song of Evil
    c. Song of the Pearl
    d. Song of Lamenting

The Pearl Multiple Choice Unit Test 2 Page 5

IV. VOCABULARY - Match the correct definitions to the words.

___ 1. Reassuring   a. climbed with effort or clumsily

___ 2. Merged   b. beat about; moved about violently

___ 3. Abandoned   c. able to be detected by the senses

___ 4. Resinous   d. covered over

___ 5. Clambered   e. restoring to confidence

___ 6. Precipitated   f. that which is left after part is taken away

___ 7. Lucent   g. a solid or semi-solid substance from a plant

___ 8. Incandescence   h. shining, giving off light

___ 9. Prophecy   i. shining brilliantly

___ 10. Remote   j. tired or worn out

___ 11. Perplexed   k. vigorous

___ 12. Frantically   l. prediction

___ 13. Weary   m. joined together

___ 14. Threshed   n. distant or secluded

___ 15. Residue   o. gave up, deserted

___ 16. Obscured   p. created

___ 17. Poultice   q. troubled with uncertainty

___ 18. Discontentedly r. with dissatisfaction

___ 19. Perceptible   s. wild with anger

___ 20. Strenuous   t. a hot moist mass of herbs

ANSWER SHEET - *The Pearl*
Multiple Choice Unit Tests

I. Matching	II. Multiple Choice	IV. Vocabulary
1. ___	1. ___	1. ___
2. ___	2. ___	2. ___
3. ___	3. ___	3. ___
4. ___	4. ___	4. ___
5. ___	5. ___	5. ___
6. ___	6. ___	6. ___
7. ___	7. ___	7. ___
8. ___	8. ___	8. ___
9. ___	9. ___	9. ___
10. ___	10. ___	10. ___
11. ___	11. ___	11. ___
12. ___	12. ___	12. ___
13. ___	13. ___	13. ___
14. ___	14. ___	14. ___
15. ___		15. ___
16. ___		16. ___
		17. ___
		18. ___
		19. ___
		20. ___

ANSWER KEY MULTIPLE CHOICE UNIT TESTS – *The Pearl*

Answers to Unit Test 1 are in the left column. Answers to Unit Test 2 are in the right column.

I. Matching	II. Multiple Choice	IV. Vocabulary
1. I J	1. A C	1. G E
2. E B	2. D D	2. K M
3. D E	3. D A	3. A O
4. J H	4. A B	4. M G
5. H I	5. D C	5. I A
6. G F	6. B A	6. D P
7. F C	7. A D	7. J H
8. A G	8. D C	8. H I
9. C A	9. C B	9. O L
10. B D	10. D B	10. F N
11. K L	11. A B	11. N Q
12. L M	12. B C	12. R S
13. M K	13. D B	13. Q J
14. L M	14. B D	14. B B
15. L M		15. T F
16. K L		16. P D
		17. E T
		18. L R
		19. C C
		20. S K

UNIT RESOURCE MATERIALS

BULLETIN BOARD IDEAS - *The Pearl*

1. Save one corner of the board for the best of students' *The Pearl* writing assignments.

2. Take one of the word search puzzles from the extra activities packet and with a marker copy it over in a large size on the bulletin board. Write the clue words to find to one side. Invite students prior to and after class to find the words and circle them on the bulletin board.

3. Write several of the most significant quotations from the book onto the board on brightly colored paper.

4. Make a bulletin board listing the vocabulary words for this unit. As you complete sections of the novel and discuss the vocabulary for each section, write the definitions on the bulletin board. (If your board is one students face frequently, it will help them learn the words.)

5. Bring in (or have students bring in) pictures of village fishing life from magazines. Make a collage if you have enough different pictures (or post individual pictures on colorful paper if you only have a few).

6. Title the board "THE PEARL: A STORY OF GOOD VERSUS EVIL." Post pictures of obviously good things symbolized in the story (family, homes, traditions) on one side of the board, and obviously bad things symbolized in the story (greed, corruption, self-interest) on the other side of the board.

7. Title the board "THE PEARL: THE STORY OF ONE MAN'S DREAM." Find pictures of advertisements for the lottery or sweepstakes and post them on one side of the board. On the other side, place pictures of the things people might dream of owning or doing with their fortunes.

8. Title the board "THE PEARL: MAN VERSUS SOCIETY." Post pictures and articles about people who have "fought city hall."

9. See Lesson One for the bulletin board introductory activity.

EXTRA ACTIVITIES

One of the difficulties in teaching a novel is that all students don't read at the same speed. One student who likes to read may take the book home and finish it in a day or two. Sometimes a few students finish the in-class assignments early. The problem, then, is finding suitable extra activities for students.

The best thing I've found is to keep a little library in the classroom. For this unit on *The Pearl*, you might check out from the school library other related books and articles about diving, boating, careers in the seafood industry, gemstone industry or medical professions, people who have become rich overnight, doctors and the medical professions, or articles of criticism about *The Pearl*. A biography of John Steinbeck would be interesting for some students to read. Other works by John Steinbeck would also make good additions to your in-class library.

Other things you may keep on hand are puzzles. I have made some relating directly to *The Pearl* for you. Feel free to duplicate them.

Some students may like to draw. You might devise a contest or allow some extra-credit grade for students who draw characters or scenes from *The Pearl*. Note, too, that if the students do not want to keep their drawings you may pick up some extra bulletin board materials this way. If you have a contest and you supply the prize (a CD or something like that perhaps), you could, possibly, make the drawing itself a non-refundable entry fee.

The pages which follow contain games, puzzles and worksheets. The keys, when appropriate, immediately follow the puzzle or worksheet. There are two main groups of activities: one group for the unit; that is, generally relating to the *Pearl* text, and another group of activities related strictly to the *Pearl* vocabulary.

Directions for these games, puzzles and worksheets are self-explanatory. The object here is to provide you with extra materials you may use in any way you choose.

MORE ACTIVITIES - *The Pearl*

1. Pick a chapter or scene and have the students act it out on a stage. (Perhaps you could assign various scenes to different groups of students so more than one scene could be acted and more students could participate.)

2. Read *The Monkey's Paw* and compare and contrast it with *The Pearl*.

3. Use some of the related topics noted earlier in the unit as topics for guest speakers or research papers.

4. Have students design a book cover (front and back and inside flaps) for *The Pearl*.

5. Have students design a bulletin board (ready to be put up; not just sketched) for *The Pearl*.

6. Have students choose songs they know as representative of the songs in the story. Let students bring in their songs and play them for the class. Perhaps have a contest to see who brings in the best song for each of the songs in the book.

7. Have students research, compare and contrast, cost and coverage of two medical plans for a family of four.

8. Kino was going to use part of his fortune for Coyotito's education. How much does education cost today? Have students find out how much their local governments spend on education and how much four years of college education costs.

9. Pretend Kino is charged with murder and hold a trial when he comes back into town.

10. Have students find out exactly what the odds are of finding a pearl or winning the lottery or winning a sweepstakes.

11. Have a gemstone merchant visit your class to discuss the kinds of stones that are valuable, how valuable they are, what makes one better than another, how they are processed, etc.

WORD SEARCH - *The Pearl*

All words in this list are associated with *The Pearl*. The words are placed backwards, forward, diagonally, up and down. The included words are listed below.

```
J Q B F Q B P K M Z S D J Y R T J Y R G G B R S
F B T A B P G A X C T R S W N Z G U W O O R Y Z
Q H X G B V R S T D N C E E V G R B A N T O Y Z
S T N L C Y F I S H O N I K N I F E O N A C D S
K M I L L L J U R K C C L C X V S T X A I O B
C V V I U X F T P H S E N W F A G M X S B M M D
E A M G B J D I A I B W S M C N R M V P Y P T G
X A P M V A O N N N C R N G O R O T V V O O S X
F S Y I M N D M I R E O G S S U W C D U W N J H
I X J G T K O E W Y O W W L G Z N H L N W Y N N
E N Y Q K A T Z U P R I E S T L Q T S T C O S Q
J D S X L S L B R S E S Q W Q D I P A N T A W S
N C U T T F D A V R R A Q X T C E P X I M Z R N
L W C C I F H J H F V F R G E O X Q T O N Q H G
Q S X D A N O V E L L A H L P R Z O T W X G K K
P Y H H S T C G V M X J B L N Z Y N C X B G G W
S D T T Q N I T P X P B E R X O A Z G S M C V B
F L R V C F P O R V L S M C C U Q B G S P Y P F
N G F T F Z B C N B G R H V J J Y J W F Z X Q G
V S W S N K W F T X C K R B Q X X G G K X N P Q
```

BABY	EDUCATION	JUANA	PEARL
BAD	EVIL	JUANTOMAS	POULTICE
BID	FAMILY	KINO	PRIEST
BUYERS	FISH	KNIFE	SCORPION
CANOE	GOOD	MAN	SONGS
CAPITAL	GULF	MOUNTAIN	STEINBECK
CAVE	HAND	NOVELLA	TOWNSPEOPLE
CONFLICT	HARPOON	OMNISCIENT	TRACKERS
COYOTITO	HUT	OYSTER	
DOCTOR	INSTINCT	PATH	

CROSSWORD - *The Pearl*

CROSSWORD CLUES - *The Pearl*

ACROSS

2. He is attacked by a scorpion
5. Fisherman's weapon Kino hopes to buy
10. Kino's wife
12. --- of Kino's find spread quickly in the town
13. Place Kino hopes to sell the pearl
14. Not ever
15. Also
16. I am the _____
17. Joined together
18. He finds the pearl
19. Trade for money
23. The pearl gave him ideas of church repairs
26. Married to an uncle
28. Close to
30. Symbolic of the natural way of the universe
34. Music in the story
36. _____ vs. Evil
37. Kino's find which holds his hopes for the future
40. Expression of deep sorrow by weeping or wailing
43. Seaweed pack on Coyotito's wound
45. Refused to treat Coyotito at first
46. Beat about; moved about violently
47. Distant or secluded
48. Too great a desire to have wealth and riches
49. Man vs. Society, for example

DOWN

1. Kino injuries his on the doctor's gate
2. Symbol of tradition, the old way of life
3. Natural home of the Pearl
4. One kills Coyotito; Kino kills them
5. Kino's house, symbol of good and tradition
6. Turn over
7. A point of view
8. Short novel
9. The buyers should have offered Kino ---- money
10. Kino's brother
11. Song of the _____, a song of happiness and harmony
20. They fix the market and cheat the villagers
21. Place Kino is attacked and kills a man
22. Kino's weapon against the intruder
24. Song of _____, a song of bad things
25. They all think of the riches the pearl could bring them
27. A little travel
29. Animal intuition
31. It attacked Coyotito
32. Kino's dream for Coyotito
33. Kind of luck the Pearl brings Kino's family
35. Final resting place of the pearl
38. Place where Coyotito is killed
39. Tired or worn out
41. The inward nature of anything
42. Competitive offer to purchase something
44. Shining, giving off light

CROSSWORD ANSWER KEY - *The Pearl*

MATCHING QUIZ/WORKSHEET 1 - *The Pearl*

___ 1. CANOE   A. Seaweed pack on Coyotito's wound

___ 2. MOUNTAIN   B. Animal intuition

___ 3. FISH   C. Competitive offer to purchase something

___ 4. INSTINCT   D. Author

___ 5. MAN   E. He finds the pearl

___ 6. JUANA   F. Kino's wife

___ 7. POULTICE   G. Final resting place of the pearl

___ 8. KINO   H. Song of _____, a song of bad things

___ 9. PRIEST   I. Short novel

___ 10. BID   J. They all think of the riches the pearl could bring them

___ 11. GULF   K. Place to which Kino, Juana and Coyotito flee

___ 12. JUAN TOMAS   L. I am the _____

___ 13. BAD   M. Kino's brother

___ 14. SCORPION   N. It attacked Coyotito

___ 15. STEINBECK   O. Symbol of tradition, the old way of life

___ 16. EVIL   P. Symbolic of the natural way of the universe

___ 17. NOVELLA   Q. A point of view

___ 18. OMNISCIENT   R. Place Kino is attacked and kills a man

___ 19. TOWNSPEOPLE   S. Kind of luck the Pearl brings Kino's family

___ 20. PATH   T. The pearl gave him ideas of church repairs

MATCHING QUIZ/WORKSHEET 2 - *The Pearl*

___ 1. JUANA   A. Final resting place of the pearl

___ 2. COYOTITO   B. A point of view

___ 3. EDUCATION   C. Natural home of the Pearl

___ 4. CANOE   D. Short novel

___ 5. DOCTOR   E. Kino's weapon against the intruder

___ 6. MOUNTAIN   F. Refused to treat Coyotito at first

___ 7. INSTINCT   G. Kino's wife

___ 8. MAN   H. It attacked Coyotito

___ 9. KNIFE   I. Fisherman's weapon Kino hopes to buy

___10. NOVELLA   J. Symbol of tradition, the old way of life

___11. BUYERS   K. They fix the market and cheat the Villagers

___12. SCORPION   L. I am the _____

___13. FISH   M. Place to which Kino, Juana and Coyotito flee

___14. CONFLICT   N. Animal intuition

___15. GULF   O. Seaweed pack on Coyotito's wound

___16. CAPITAL   P. He is attacked by a scorpion

___17. POULTICE   Q. Symbolic of the natural way of the universe

___18. OMNISCIENT   R. Kino's dream for Coyotito

___19. OYSTER   S. Place Kino hopes to sell the pearl

___20. HARPOON   T. Man vs. Society, for example

KEY: MATCHING QUIZ/WORKSHEETS - *The Pearl*

Worksheet 1
1. O
2. K
3. P
4. B
5. L
6. F
7. A
8. E
9. T
10. C
11. G
12. M
13. S
14. N
15. D
16. H
17. I
18. Q
19. J
20. R

Worksheet 2
1. G
2. P
3. R
4. J
5. F
6. M
7. N
8. L
9. E
10. D
11. K
12. H
13. Q
14. T
15. A
16. S
17. O
18. B
19. C
20. I

JUGGLE LETTER REVIEW GAME CLUE SHEET - *The Pearl*

SCRAMBLED	WORD	CLUE
ATS NMJUOA	JUAN TOMAS	Kino's brother
VLNOAEL	NOVELLA	Short novel
RONPOCIS	SCORPION	It attacked Coyotito
IUTEOPLC	POULTICE	Seaweed pack on Coyotito's wound
VELI	EVIL	Song of _____, a song of bad things
YOTOOTCI	COYOTITO	He is attacked by a scorpion
ADB	BAD	Kind of luck the Pearl brings Kino's family
OTNAEDCUI	EDUCATION	Kino's dream for Coyotito
HFIS	FISH	Symbolic of the natural way of the universe
STERACKR	TRACKERS	One kills Coyotito; Kills them
NRAOHOP	HARPOON	Fisherman's weapon Kino hopes to buy
RDOCTO	DOCTOR	Refused to treat Coyotito at first
NMA	MAN	I am the _____
NCBTEEKSI	STEINBECK	Author
CIINSTTN	INSTINCT	Animal intuition
UTH	HUT	Kino's house, symbol of good and tradition
IEKNF	KNIFE	Kino's weapon against the intruder
HPAT	PATH	Place Kino is attacked and kills a man
ESTRYO	OYSTER	Natural home of the Pearl
NIOSEMTCIN	OMNISCIENT	A point of view

VOCABULARY RESOURCE MATERIALS

VOCABULARY WORD SEARCH - *The Pearl*

All words in this list are associated with *The Pearl* with an emphasis on the vocabulary words chosen for study in the text. The words are placed backwards, forward, diagonally, up and down. The included words are listed below.

```
R U P T U R E Y E D H Q P M E D V Z L V D Y F B
D X Q Y J Y X L M X I G E E X T E V X U R J H X
D X X D L G L E T E H S N U T V O R V A C Z V K
C E A S E L E S S U O I C I D U J M E R G E D P
D S H B N X A S U N C B L O D I L W E B C C N G
L E T S A L E C R O E O S A N O S A R R M C G T
P A T Y E N M L I E N C M C R T O E N Q Y A Q S
P E M A C R D R P T A O S P U A E R R T R F L F
C O R E T R H O J R N S T E A R T N B M B V K C
A P U C N I P T N O E A S O D R E I T B Z W Q Y
S V R L E T P C L E X P R U N N A D O E X S V W
L P A O T P F I V G D V W F R O A B Y N D W H T
T G X R P I T V C S V Q K W Y I M C L C B L R N
V F H D I H C I R E S I N O U S N J N E P J Y V
F G C C I C E E B R R H Y G S T Y G S I W W H G
G D M C H W E C H L D P L S T R E N U O U S R G
L E T H A R G Y Y L E V I S N E H E R P P A H R
```

ABANDONED	EXHILARATION	MONOTONOUSLY	REMOTE
APPREHENSIVELY	FRANTICALLY	OBSCURED	RESIDUE
AVARICE	JUDICIOUS	PERCEPTIBLE	RESINOUS
BROODING	LAMENT	PERPLEXED	RUPTURE
CEASELESS	LETHARGY	PETULANT	STRENUOUS
CLAMBERED	LETHARGY	POULTICE	THRESHED
COMPARABLE	LUCENT	PRECIPITATED	WEARY
DISCONTENTEDLY	MERGED	PROPHECY	
ESSENCE	MONOLITHIC	REASSURING	

VOCABULARY CROSSWORD - *The Pearl*

VOCABULARY CROSSWORD CLUES - *The Pearl*

ACROSS
3. Joined together
5. Unceasing, continual
9. Song of _____, a song of bad things
12. Gave up, deserted
14. Prediction
15. Angry
18. The pearl gave him ideas of church repairs
19. Climbed with effort or clumsily
21. That which is left after part is taken away
22. Single; alone
24. Tired or worn out
25. Impatient or irritable
27. Symbol of tradition, the old way of life
28. He finds the pearl
29. Sometimes electric, snake-like sea creature
30. Get away quickly on foot
31. Place Kino is attacked and kills a man
33. Music in the store
34. Seeing organ
37. Like resin, a semi-solid plant substance
38. Kind of luck the Pearl brings Kino's family
39. Allow
40. Cut tree trunk
41. Song of the _____, a song of happiness and harmony
42. Final resting place of the pearl
43. Liberated; unconfined

44. Troubled with uncertainty
45. Kino's house, symbol of good and tradition
46. Summed together
47. Revise

DOWN
1. --- Pearl
2. The inward nature of anything
4. Distant or secluded
6. Too great a desire to have wealth and riches
7. They fix the market and cheat the villagers
8. Similar
10. Shining brilliantly
11. Beat about; moved about violently
12. Uneasily; fearfully
13. With dissatisfaction
16. Concealing under a false appearance
17. Expression of deep sorrow by weeping or wailing
20. Thinking about same thing in a distressed way
23. Wild with anger
25. Able to be detected by the senses
26. A condition of abnormal drowsiness
32. Covered over
35. Kino's weapon against the intruder
36. Shining, giving off light
41. Symbolic of the natural way of the universe
42. _____ vs. Evil

VOCABULARY CROSSWORD ANSWER KEY - *The Pearl*

		T								E		M	E	R	G	E	D	
		H			C	E	A	S	E	L	E	S	S		E			B
C		E	V	I	L		V			S			M		T			U
O				N	A	B	A	N	D	O	N	E	D		P	R	O	P	H	E	C	Y
M	A	D		C		P		R		I		N		L		T		R		E
P	I		A		P	R	I	E	S	T		C	L	A	M	B	E	R	E	D	R
A	S		N		R		C		C			E		M		R		S		S
R	E	S	I	D	U	E		E		O	N	E			E		O		H		F
A	E		E		H				N				N		O		W	E	A	R	Y
B	M		S		E		P	E	T	U	L	A	N	T		D			D		A
L	B		C	A	N	O	E		E				K	I	N	G				N
E	L		E		S		R	U	N				N			P	A	T	H
	I		N		I		C		T		H		O		G			I	
S	O	N	G	S		V		E	Y	E		A		B		K		L		C
		G		E		E		P		D		R	E	S	I	N	O	U	S	B	A	D
						L	E	T		L	O	G		C		I		C		L
	F	A	M	I	L	Y		I		Y		Y		U		F		E		G	U	L	F
	I						B				F	R	E	E		N		O		Y
	S		P	E	R	P	L	E	X	E	D		E			T		O
	H	U	T				E		A	D	D	E	D		E	D	I	T

VOCABULARY WORKSHEET 1 - *The Pearl*

___ 1. Covered over
    a. Merged   b. Incandescence   c. Resinous   d. Obscured

___ 2. The inward nature of anything
    a. Lament   b. Essence   c. Frantically   d. Incandescence

___ 3. A sold or semi-sold substance from a plant
    a. Weary   b. Monotonously   c. Dissembling   d. Resinous

___ 4. Impatient or irritable
    a. Undulating   b. Ceaseless   c. Petulant   d. Merged

___ 5. Expression of deep sorrow by weeping or wailing
    a. Coagulating   b. Lament   c. Transfigured   d. Discontentedly

___ 6. Joined together
    a. Transfigured   b. Remote   c. Resinous   d. Merged

___ 7. Tired or worn out
    a. Incandescence   b. Weary   c. Abandoned   d. Coagulating

___ 8. Gave up, deserted
    a. Obscured   b. Abandoned   c. Coagulating   d. Perplexed

___ 9. Going in same tone without variation
    a. Apprehensively   b. Comparable   c. Monotonously   d. Contemptuously

___10. Created
    a. Dissembling   b. Precipitated   c. Residue   d. Lucent

___11. A condition of abnormal drowsiness
    a. Avarice   b. Judicious   c. Lethargy   d. Perceptible

___12. Wise and careful
    a. Monolithic   b. Resinous   c. Poultice   d. Judicious

___13. Shining, giving off light
    a. Petulant   b. Lucent   c. Discontentedly   d. Strenuous

___14. To keep thinking about same thing in a distressed way
    a. Perceptible   b. Ceaseless   c. Brooding   d. Reassuring

___15. Crack; hole
    a. Undulating   b. Reassuring   c. Perplexed   d. Rupture

___16. Becoming a soft semi-solid mass
    a. Avarice   b. Coagulating   c. Rupture   d. Monolithic

___17. Beat about; moved about violently
    a. Threshed   b. Poultice   c. Weary   d. Exhilaration

___18. Able to be detected by the senses
    a. Perceptible   b. Poultice   c. Rupture   d. Abandoned

___19. Made of a single block of stone
    a. Lucent   b. Lethargy   c. Reassuring   d. Monolithic

___20. Vigorous
    a. Weary   b. Strenuous   c. Comparable   d. Undulating

VOCABULARY WORKSHEET 2 - *The Pearl*

___ 1. LETHARGY   A. uneasily, fearfully

___ 2. CLAMBERED   B. prediction

___ 3. AVARICE   C. tired or worn out

___ 4. RUPTURE   D. wise and careful

___ 5. JUDICIOUS   E. shining, giving off light

___ 6. PETULANT   F. expression of deep sorrow by weeping or wailing

___ 7. CEASELESS   G. impatient or irritable

___ 8. APPREHENSIVELY   H. wild with anger

___ 9. PROPHECY   I. shining brilliantly

___10. MONOTONOUSLY   J. crack; hole

___11. LAMENT   K. joined together

___12. RESINOUS   L. like resin, a semi-solid plant substance

___13. WEARY   M. unceasing, continual

___14. LUCENT   N. troubled with uncertainty

___15. PRECIPITATED   O. created

___16. DISCONTENTEDLY   P. going in same tone without variation

___17. INCANDESCENCE   Q. too great a desire to have wealth and riches

___18. FRANTICALLY   R. a condition of abnormal drowsiness

___19. PERPLEXED   S. with dissatisfaction

___20. MERGED   T. climbed with effort or clumsily

KEY: VOCABULARY WORKSHEETS - *The Pearl*

Worksheet 1	Worksheet 2
1. D	1. R
2. B	2. T
3. D	3. Q
4. C	4. J
5. B	5. D
6. D	6. G
7. B	7. M
8. B	8. A
9. C	9. B
10. B	10. P
11. C	11. F
12. D	12. L
13. B	13. C
14. C	14. E
15. D	15. O
16. B	16. S
17. A	17. I
18. A	18. H
19. D	19. N
20. B	20. K

VOCABULARY JUGGLE LETTER REVIEW GAME CLUES - *The Pearl*

SCRAMBLED	WORD	CLUE
XEARALIONIHT	EXHILARATION	a feeling of high spirits
ACFYLTNIARL	FRANTICALLY	wild with anger
AHELGTYR	LETHARGY	a condition of abnormal drowsiness
ENECSES	ESSENCE	the inward nature of anything
ALPOBERMCA	COMPARABLE	similar
ETLIUCOP	POULTICE	a hot moist mass of herbs
NATFDGSRIURE	TRANSFIGURED	changed in outward appearance
NICHIMOTLO	MONOLITHIC	made of a single block of stone
TPEEIERPLBC	PERCEPTIBLE	able to be detected by the senses
RAWYE	WEARY	tired or worn out
YMSNOOTLNOOU	MONOTONOUSLY	going in same tone without variation
ANUGNTIULD	UNDULATING	to cause to move in waves
AADNBNEOD	ABANDONED	gave up, deserted
ONGOIDBR	BROODING	to keep thinking about same thing in a distressed way
EMDERG	MERGED	joined together
CEINSASDNCNEE	INCANDESCENCE	shining brilliantly
GLCUAGIOTAN	COAGULATING	becoming a soft semi-solid mass
EUBDRCSO	OBSCURED	covered over
SNIUOSER	RESINOUS	like resin, a semi-solid plant substance
EAUNTPTL	PETULANT	impatient or irritable